Guide with reconstructions

PETRA

past & present

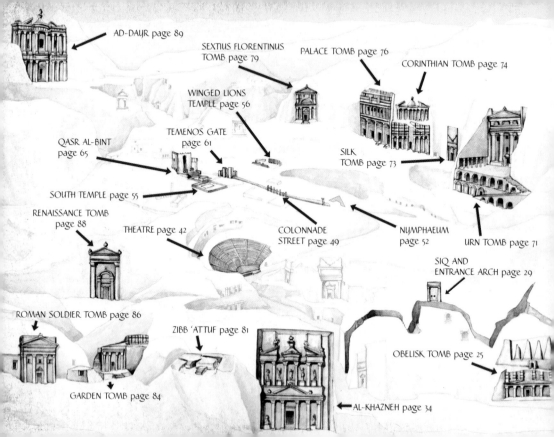

AD-DAYR page 89

SEXTIUS FLORENTINUS TOMB page 79

PALACE TOMB page 76

CORINTHIAN TOMB page 74

WINGED LIONS TEMPLE page 56

QASR AL-BINT page 65

TEMENOS GATE page 61

SILK TOMB page 73

SOUTH TEMPLE page 55

RENAISSANCE TOMB page 88

THEATRE page 42

COLONNADE STREET page 49

NYMPHAEUM page 52

URN TOMB page 71

SIQ AND ENTRANCE ARCH page 29

ROMAN SOLDIER TOMB page 86

ZIBB 'ATTUF page 81

OBELISK TOMB page 25

GARDEN TOMB page 84

AL-KHAZNEH page 34

Petra stands at an elevation of about 900 meters in the midst of the vast plateau stretching eastward from the Dead Sea and the Wadi al-Arabah, the deep crevice through which the River Jordan once flowed into the Gulf of Aqaba. The archaeological site, situated about 300 kilometers south of Amman, can be reached today using the modern road known as the "Desert Way", or the more suggestive Kings' Road, which follows the original course of the ancient road of the same name.

The city of Petra, now far from the major traffic arteries, was once situated at the crossroads between the most important caravan trade routes, at the point where the trails coming from southern and eastern Arabia continued on toward the Mediterranean Sea and crossed the Kings' Road, which connected Syria to Egypt through Transjordan and the Sinai Penin-

Basalt inscribed stone with hunting scene, 4th Century BC. (Amman, Archaeological Museum)

sula. Petra built its fortune on the control of the caravan routes and the monopoly the Nabatean traders commanded over the transport of luxury goods passing through the area. The incense and myrrh coming from southwestern Arabia, the spices, fabrics, and precious stones arriving from India and China to the ports of eastern Arabia and, lastly, the bitumen produced in the Dead Sea were transported to Petra and dispatched from there to the major Mediterranean markets through the emporiums of Gaza and Rhinocolura (el-'Arish) on the Palestinian coast and Aila (Aqaba) on the Arabian coast of the Red Sea. The Nabatean traders not only handled the organization of the transport, exploiting the formidable capacity for resistance of dromedaries, but they held customs rights over the goods in transit which could arrive as high as 25% of their value.

The ancient city of Petra lies in the canyon carved out by the so-called "River of Moses", which gave the modern village of Wadi Musa its name. The rocky conformation of the landscape is the origin of the city's ancient name: in fact, Petra is the Greek translation of Sela (which means "rock" in Hebrew), the name by which the city is

Limestone strata of the rock walls around Petra

called in the Bible; on the other hand, the Nabateans called their capital city "Reqem". The modern name of "Rose-Red City" derives from the splendid shades of color – dominated by pink or yellow, depending on the time of day, but streaked with white, grey, blue, and red – that characterize the sandstone layers into which the monuments of Petra are carved.

The city is surrounded on all sides by rocky massifs (*jabal*), separated by deep gorges carved out by season-

al streams of water (*wadi*), and easily accessible only on the eastern side through a narrow passage opened and formed through the centuries by the erosive action of the Wadi Musa. Beyond this gorge, known as Siq, the Wadi Musa valley widens into a large canyon delimited to the east by Jabal al-Khubtha, to the south by the Zibb 'Attuf and Jabal al-Katuta, and to the west by the al-Habis massif and Jabal ad-Dayr. It is here that the monumental center of the city stands with its public, civil, and religious buildings, while the surrounding mountain slopes form a crown of dwellings carved into the rock.

Outside of the city of the living, along the deep gorges dug by the Wadi Musa and its main tributaries – Wadi al-Farasa and Wadi Thughra to the south, Wadi Abu 'Ullayqa and Wadi Mataha to the north – stretch the vast rupestrian necropolises to which Petra's fame is most tied. Thanks to the presence of perpetual springs and

Rock dwelling in the wall in front of the theatre

an advanced plumbing system, the city, a semidesert today, was once a thriving center luxuriant with blooming gardens and cultivated fields.

In the late 1st century BC the Greek geographer Strabo described the city as follows:

"The metropolis of the Nabateans, Petra, is located on a site that is flat and leveled, but surrounded all around by rocks; the external part of the site is steep, while the internal part is rich with springs used both for household purposes and for watering the gardens. Outside of the rocky circuit, most of the territory is desert, in particular that toward Judea."

The tombs carved into the bedrock in outer Siq

The most ancient traces of habitation of the area around Petra date back to the Paleolithic, specifically to the 11th millennium BC. It was, however, only starting with the Neolithic (8500-4000 BC) that actual settlements began to develop, with a coexistence of sedentary communities devoted to farming and groups of nomadic shepherds. The most important of these settlements is the village of al-Beidha, situated a few kilometers north of Petra, where round- and rectangular-plan dwellings, millstones for grinding wheat, and tombs were discovered. During the Bronze Age (3200-1200 BC), the settlements of southern Jordan were abandoned, perhaps because of changes in the climate, and the area of Petra was reoccupied only in around 1500 BC by the population of the Horites, who lived in the caves on the mountainsides.

In around 1200 BC, the area to the east of the Dead Sea was occupied by the Semitic people called the Edomites. The independent state of Edom soon clashed with the kingdom of David (ca. 1000 BC) and continued to compete down through the following centuries with the kingdoms of Israel and Judah, created from the division of the kingdom of Solomon.

Jug in the shape of a bird, from Jericho, 1800-1550 BC. (Amman, Archaeological Museum)

During the period of their maximum splendor (8th-7th century BC), the Edomites created the first permanent settlement in the area of the future city of Petra. The Edomite village was situated on the Umm al-Biyara massif, which dominated the Wadi Musa valley to the southwest, and consisted of simple stone dwellings and plastered cisterns. It is precisely from these cisterns that the mountain's name was taken: in fact, Umm al-Biyara means "mother of cisterns".

During the 6th century BC, perhaps as a result of the impoverishment and depopulation caused by the Babylonian conquest, the Edomites were replaced by the Nabateans, a nomad population of Arab origin and Aramaic language, devoted to shepherding and caravan trading. Between the 6th and 5th century BC, the Nabateans settled in the Edomite village of Umm al-Biyara: the privileged position at the crossroads of the most important caravan routes, the natural defense offered by the rocky massifs ands crags and, lastly, the great availability of water made Petra the ideal site for the capital city of the new Nabatean kingdom.

The first historic accounts of the city date from 312 BC, when Antigonus Monophthalmus, a general and successor of Alexander the Great, twice attempted to conquer Petra and seize the riches held there. The two attacks waged by Antigonus failed because of the valorous resistance of the Nabateans, who barricaded themselves amidst the impregnable rocks of Umm al-Biyara. In his narration of these events, Greek historian Diodorus Siculus described the customs of the Nabateans for the first time:

"For the sake of those who do not know, it will be useful to state in some detail the customs of those Arabs,

y following which it is believed, they preserve their liberty. They live in the open air, claiming as native land a wilderness that has neither rivers nor abundant springs. It is their custom neither to plant grain, set out any fruit-bearing tree, use wine, nor construct any house. Some of them raise camels, others sheep, pasturing them in the desert. While there are many Arabian tribes who use the desert as pasture the Nabateans far surpass the others in wealth although they are not much more than ten thousand in number; for not a few of them are accustomed to bring down to the sea frankincense and myrrh and the most costly of spices , which they procure from those who convey them from what is called Arabia Felix. They are exceptionally fond of freedom; and whenever a strong force of enemies comes near, they take refuge in the desert, using this as a fortress; for it lacks water and cannot be crossed by others, but to them alone, since they have prepared subterranean reservoirs lined with stucco, it furnishes safety."

Through the following centuries, the Nabateans managed to maintain their

Head of the god Qos from the Nabatean sanctuary of Khirbet Tannur (Amman, Archaeological Museum)

10

ndependence in spite of the repeated attacks by the Ptolemies and the Seleucids, who ruled over the neighboring Hellenistic states of Egypt and Syria; they were thus able to create a kingdom that, at the end of the 3rd century BC, comprised Transjordan, the Palestinian Negev desert, and the fertile Syrian region of Hauran. Benefiting from the prosperity achieved thanks to its growing control over the caravan trade, during this period the village of Petra became a permanent settlement, and was moved from the top of Umm al-Biyara to the Wadi Musa valley, where simple cobblestone and clay dwellings were built.

Nabatean inscription in honour of king Aretas IV, 10 BC. (Amman, Archaeological Museum)

The next historic information on the Nabatean capital dates from the first half of the 2nd century BC. In fact, the Bible mentions that in 168 BC the Nabateans, previously organized as a confederation of tribes under the control of a sheik, were governed by a king named Aretas (conventionally called Aretas I), whose residence was at Petra. Taking advantage of the decline of the Seleucid monarchy, Aretas I and his unknown successors consolidated the Nabatean kingdom, gaining a position of supremacy over sea trade as well, thanks to the control of the emporiums of Gaza and Leuke Kome (today's Aynunah), situated on the Palestinian coast of the Mediterranean and the Arabian shore of the Red Sea, respectively. The reaction of the Ptolemies and the Hasmoneans, who in the meantime had come to power in Judea, was not late in coming: during the reign of Aretas II (ca. 120-96 BC) an Egyptian fleet defeated the Nabatean ships in the Red Sea, while in 100 BC the king of Judea, Alexander Jannaeus, succeeded in seizing the port of Gaza. In spite of these defeats, during the time of Obodas I (95-86 BC) and Aretas III Philhellene (85-62 BC.), the Nabatean kingdom rose rapidly and reached its maximum extension, arriving at comprising southern Syria and northern Arabia.

In 64 BC the action of the Roman general Pompey ended the Seleucid monarchy and led to the creation of the province of Syria. After having intervened in the dynastic conflict which broke out in Judea, Pompey tried in vain to extend his supremacy over the Nabateans; similar attempts made in the following years by the Roman legates of Syria Aemilius Scaurus and Aulus Gabinius were also unsuccessful. During the late 1st century BC, Obodas II (62-59 BC) and Malichus I (59-

30 BC), working their way with skillful diplomacy amongst the rivals in the Roman civil wars, succeeded in guaranteeing the survival of the kingdom; in exchange for their independence, the Nabatean kings promised to pay Rome a tribute and to accept the condition of client kings. However, during the period from 35 to 31 BC, the Nabatean kingdom lost part of its territory, which was given as a gift by Antony to Cleopatra.

For the Nabatean kingdom, as for the other regions of the Near and Middle East, Octavian's victory at Actium in 31 BC marked the beginning of an age of peace and prosperity. The pacification of the eastern Mediterranean after decades of uninterrupted conflicts made it possible to fully reactivate the land routes connecting Arabia with the Mediter-

Nabatean painted bowls, 1st century AD.
(Amman, Archaeological Museum)

ranean. At the same time, the discovery of the monsoon regime facilitated sea communications between the Far East and the Arabian Peninsula. The Nabateans, who by now held the monopoly of the organization of the caravan trade, were among the main beneficiaries of this political and economic upswing.

Starting with this period, which corresponds to the kingdom of Obodas III (30-9 BC), Petra experienced a period of intense urban planning and architectural development, stimulated by the numerous artistic and cultural influences arriving from the nearby Hellenistic centers, in particular from Alexandria, Egypt. The Wadi Musa valley, previously occupied by modest dwellings, was totally renovated to receive the city's monumental center; the urban perimeter was delimited with the construction of fortresses where there was no natural rock protection; lastly, vast hydraulic engineering works were undertaken to ensure the city's water supply and the irrigation of the surrounding fields. It was, however, mainly during the first half of the 1st century AD, under the rule of Aretas IV (9 BC-40 AD), that Petra was enriched with sumptuous public, religious, and funerary buildings; and during this period the population in the Nabatean capital reached 30,000-40,000 inhabitants, rivaling the most important metropolises of the East in cultural vitality.

Nabatean painted amphora, 2nd century AD. (Amman, Archaeological Museum)

Just as Petra's ascent had been tied to the fate and fortunes of the caravan trade, so was its decline. Starting in the second half of the 1st century AD, at the time of Malichus II (40-70 AD) and Rabbel II (70-106 AD), the axis of the caravan trade began to shift toward the frontier of the Euphrates: the ascent of the more northern cities of Palmyra, Gerasa, and Bosra reduced the importance of Petra, which was forced to surrender its role as capital city to the latter.

The decline of the Nabatean kingdom aided the Roman conquest, which was completed in 106 AD by the emperor Trajan. The new Roman province took the name of *Arabia Petraea* in homage to the ancient Nabatean city, but the decision to have the capital in Bosra indicates the Petra had by then lost its centrality, albeit while maintaining its prestige. Nevertheless, also thanks to its position along the *Via Nova Traiana*, built in 111 AD between Bosra and Aila (Aqaba) along the route of the ancient Kings' Road, over the following years Petra enjoyed a renewed prosperity: during Trajan's time it rose to the rank of *metropolis* and was embellished with the construction of the Colonnade Street; on the occasion of the visit of the emperor Hadrian, in 129-130 AD, it was given the honorary name of *Hadrianè*. During the following decades, the city began a slow but inexorable decline; the presence of a military garrison (with which several inscriptions carved along the walls of the Siq appear to be related) and the granting of the status of a colony by the emperor Elagabalus (218-222 AD) nevertheless indicate that Petra was still a center of a certain importance during the 2nd and 3rd centuries AD.

With Diocletian's reform of the empire in 293 AD, Petra became the capital of the new province of *Palaestina Tertia* or *Salutaris*, which included southern Jordan, the Negev Desert, and the Sinai Peninsula, impoverished territories that were threatened by raids by nomadic peoples.

The fear of possible invasions was probably at the origin of the decision to erect a second protective wall around Petra, embracing a much smaller urban area than the Nabatean one. On 19 May 363 a violent earthquake hit the city, devastating many of its buildings; some, like the theatre and Qasr al-Bint, were never rebuilt. Nevertheless, Petra enjoyed a certain prosperity during the early Byzantine Age: Christianity spread quickly there, so much so that in the 4th century the city was already a bishop's seat. The shops along the Colonnade Street were rebuilt, some tombs were converted into churches and, most of all, in the 5th century a large basilica decorated with magnificent mosaics was built on the northern bank of Wadi Musa.

Devastated by a second earthquake in 551, Petra was definitively abandoned after the Arab invasion of 636. The area was briefly reoccupied during the years of the Crusades by Baldwin I, who in 1116 had several castles and blockhouses built there: Li Vaux Moise (the "Valley of Moses"), as Petra was called at the time of the Crusades, was conquered by Saladin in 1189 and later completely abandoned.

THE DISCOVERY

At the end of the 12th century, after the conclusion of the experience of the Crusades, the site of Petra remained deserted and was forgotten. Groups of Bedouins camped amongst the ruins of the ancient city and, fearing the arrival of treasure hunters, kept its existence secret for many years. The rediscovery of Petra, on 21 August 1812, was made thanks to the enterprise of the young Swiss explorer Johann Ludwig Burckhardt,

Ad-Dayr as drawn by D. Roberts

The "discoverer" of Petra, J.L. Burckhardt

sent to the Middle East by the British Foreign Office for the purpose of preparing an expedition to Africa. An expert in the Arabic language and Islamic religion, so much so that he was able to travel masquerading as an Arab sheik, Burckhardt heard about the mysterious rupestrian city during a sojourn in the nearby Crusaders' fortress of Shobak. Curious, Burckhardt succeeded in having himself accompanied to the ruins of the city, with the excuse of wanting to make a sacrifice on the tomb of Aaron, which was situated on the top of the nearby Jabal Harun.

He immediately recognized the majestic stretch of ruins as the ancient capital of the Nabateans but, in order to avoid arousing suspicion in his unknowing guide, he had to limit his visit to a quick glance. Petra's existence was revealed to the West with the publication of his travel diary, *Travels in Arabia*, published after his death in 1829. Since then, and throughout the 20th century, Petra has become the destination of uninterrupted pilgrimages by Western explorers and travelers, who have left numerous descriptions and drawings. The archaeological excavation of the site began between the late 19th and early 20th century, with the first scientific classification of Petra's monuments.

The actual digs began in 1929, and since then they have continued without interruption up to the present day; nevertheless, the archaeological study of Petra is still far from being completed.

THE NABATEAN RELIGION

The religion reflects the composite ethnic origin and the considerable aptitude of the Nabateans for receiving and incorporating the influences coming from the outside; as such, it may be defined "syncretistic", i.e. characterized by the encounter and merging of cults of different origins.

The Nabatean religion sprang from the union between the cults focusing on the heavens, natural elements, and atmospheric phenomena typical of the tribes of nomadic origin, and the cults connected with the earth and fertility characteristic of the agricultural and sedentary societies of the Middle East. An element common to both was the tendency to represent the deity in an "aniconic" form, i.e. without resorting to anthropomorphic images. During the Hellenistic and Roman times, the Nabatean religion was enriched with important cults from Syria, Egypt, and Greece, which were included in the traditional *pantheon*: the Roman conquest also determined the adoption of figural representations of the gods.

The main deity of the Nabateans was Dushara, literally "the god of the mountain of Shara", one of the many mountainous massifs rising in the area south of Petra: a representation of the local manifestation of the supreme deity of the mountain venerated by all the tribes of nomadic shepherd of the Jordanian and north-Arabian area. Dushara governed the atmospheric phenomena and the renewal of the seasonal cycles, and was thus the god of the sky, fertility, and life. Mentioned in Greek texts with the name of Orotal, Dusara or Dusares, during the Hellenistic age Dushara became the deity protecting the reigning Nabatean dynasty; as the god of fertility and life, after the Roman conquest he was assimilated into the Greek god Dionysus and took on his iconography.

The supreme goddess of the Nabateans, often associated in the cult with Dushara, is al-'Uzza, which literally means "the strong" or "the powerful", the goddess of love and life, identified with the Greek Aphrodite. With the passing of time, al-'Uzza tended to concentrate within herself the characteristics typical of other female deities, such as the Arabian Allat (i.e. "the goddess"), the Syrian Atargatis, and the Greek Tyche, the personification of fortune. The cult of al-'Uzza is often connected with astral symbols such as the moon and the plan-et Venus, and animals such as the lion and the serpent.

Alongside Dushara and al-'Uzza, the Nabatean *pantheon* included other gods of different origins. Among the male deities were Ba'al Shamin, the "lord of the heavens" of Syrian origin, and Qos, the Edomite god of the tempest, both associated with Zeus, and al-Kutba, "the scribe", a Mesopotamian deity identified in the Greek-Roman context with Hermes.

Among the female deities, in addition to Allat and Atargatis, there were Ma-

Betyl of the goddess al'Uzza with schematic eyes and nose (Petra, Archaeological Museum)

nawat, the goddess of destiny, of Arab origin, and the Egyptian goddess Isis.

The Nabateans, like all peoples of Semitic origin, customarily represented their gods in aniconic form using stones of various forms. The betyl (from the Aramaic *beth-il*, meaning "house of god"), is an imageless rectangular, triangular, conical or (more rarely) hemispherical carved or engraved stone representing the symbolic image of the deity. For the Nabateans, the betyls were sometimes enriched with elements that schematically alluded at the physiognomy of a human face, and they were often inserted into niches or aedicules intended to be stylized representations of the sanctuary where the god resided. Countless betyls of different sizes and shapes, alone or in groups, are

Panel with bust of Hermes found in the area around the Temenos Gate

carved into the rocks of Petra, particularly along the sacred roads and near sanctuaries. The images for worship kept in the sanctuaries were probably originally sacred stones. In a late-ancient text, the betyl of Dushara venerated at Petra is described thus:

"The idol is a black stone, quadrangular, aniconic; the height is four feet (1.5 meters) and the width two feet (0.60 meters). It rests on a gilded base. They offer it sacrifices and pour the blood of the victims on it. This is their libation. The gold shines throughout the temple and the offerings are numerous."

The betyl continued to be venerated even when, during the period after the Roman conquest, the deities took on an anthropomorphic appearance.
The Nabateans venerated their gods

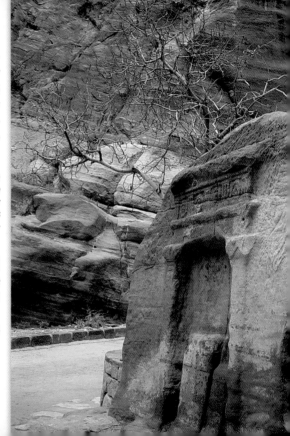

Siq, façade of an aedicule with the betyls of the gods Dushara and al'Uzza

both inside sacred buildings, the temples, and in open-air sanctuaries on mountaintops, indicated in the Bible as "high places of sacrifice".

The temples, influenced by eastern and Hellenistic models, are extremely varied in style, but they all have several elements in common; the *temenos*, i.e. the vast open area in front of the sacred building where the sacred ceremonies open to the faithful were held; the *adyton*, i.e. the most hidden part of the sanctuary, where the cult statue was kept; the *motab*, the altar or stepped platform on which the god's image was placed.

The high places of sacrifice, reachable from the city by means of steep paths that became actual "sacred ways", are open-air sanctuaries for the worship of deities that, according to the religious tradition of the Middle East, resided and manifested themselves on mountaintops. The characteristic elements of these sanctuaries were an altar for sacrifices, a betyl, and a cult triclinium, which often took the form of a simple leveled area occupied in the center by a sacred table and lined with benches. The altar was for celebrating the sacrifices in honor of the god, while the cult triclinium was used to hold the sacred banquet, during which the priests ate the remains of the sacrificed animals.

The Djinn Blocks in the valley to the east of the Siq

THE SITE

The visit to the archaeological site starts at the modern Petra Forum Rest House. Going through the wide valley that descends from the entrance toward the Siq, the first monuments of the city to be seen are funerary buildings carved out of the rock.

To the right of the road are three cubical monoliths, artificially isolated from the rock wall that closes the valley to the north, known with the name of **Djinn Blocks**, i.e. "Spirits' Blocks", because they are considered by the Bedouins the seat of the spirits guarding the city. The Djinn Blocks are between 6 and 9 meters tall and show traces of having been worked: one is

THE OBELISK TOMB AND THE BAB AL-SIQ TRICLINIUM

topped with the remains of what seems to be a pyramidal structure, and another has roughly carved semi-columns at the sides. Two of them have an internal chamber that is accessible through a small door. The Djinn Blocks are generally interpreted to be tombs either left unfinished or stripped of their original decoration; there are at least twenty other known structures of the same type in the area around Petra.

THE OBELISK TOMB
AND THE BAB AL-SIQ TRICLINIUM

A short distance ahead, to the left of the road, is an imposing complex carved out of the rock. Apparently unitary in appearance, in reality it consists of two distinct structures, the Obelisk Tomb in the upper part, and the Bab al-Siq Triclinium in the lower part.

The **Obelisk Tomb** has a simple façade, punctuated by projections and recesses and decorated with a door framed by pillars and topped with a Doric frieze. The door opens into a funeral chamber: five burial niches are carved into the walls, the most important of which, semicircular in shape, occupies the center of the back wall. Above the door is a rectangular niche, decorated with a male figure in Greek attire and flanked by the four pyramidal obelisks that give the tomb its name. In the Semitic religious tradition the soul of the deceased is represented symbolically with a commemorative monument called *nefesh* ("breath") in Aramaic, which generally takes the shape of a pyramid carved or engraved somewhere near the tomb. The four obelisks and the statue are thus the *nefesh* of the five deceased buried in the funeral chamber; it is probable that the statue represents the person buried in the central niche, perhaps the head of the family.

The **Bab al-Siq Triclinium**, carved into the lower part of the rock wall, is preceded by a courtyard cut out of the rock bank, and it has a richly decorated façade. The door is flanked by six half-columns, topped by a tympanum that opens in the center into a wide arch; the upper part is formed by an attic with dwarf pillars crowned by a broken pediment. The very simple internal chamber has benches on the three sides. A characteristic element of Nabatean funeral architecture, the triclinium was used to serve the banquets that were held each year to honor the memory of the deceased.

THE SIQ

Beyond the valley where the Djinn Blocks and Obelisk Tomb are located, the bed of the Wadi Musa shrinks to a narrow passageway between tall rock walls which today, as it has always been, is the only easy access way to the city. The gorge is called Siq, and its eastern extremity is known by the name of Bab as-Siq.

At Bab as-Siq the course of the Wadi Musa was already blocked in Nabatean times by a dike whose purpose was to prevent sudden and disastrous floodings of the river. The dike diverts the river water into an 86-meter-long tunnel called the Muthlim; the water is then conveyed through a conduit (partly carved into the rock and partly made of terracotta pipes) into the course of the Wadi Mataha, which again joins with the Wadi Musa at the start of the Colonnade Street. Thanks to the development of this ingenious water system and the presence of numerous cisterns, Petra was never without the

26

The Obelisk Tomb and the Bab al-Siq triclinium, reconstruction

water necessary for meeting the domestic needs of its inhabitants, filling the fountains and watering the gardens decorating the city, and irrigating the surrounding fields.

The gulley of the Siq, closed between rock cliffs

The access to the Siq with the traces of the arched gateway and the channel carved into the rock

At the same time as the creation of the dike, the entrance of the Siq was raised with the construction of a bridge. These works have been dated to the second half of the 1st century AD.

THE ENTRANCE ARCH TO THE SIQ

The point where the road coming from the Kings' Road enters the Siq is marked by an arched door, built at the end of the Nabatean age at the same time as the dike and the bridge. Up until the earthquake of 1896, the door was covered by a vault of stone blocks, reproduced in drawings by 19th-century travelers. The lower rows of the arch are still visible on the two rock walls that close the Siq entrance at the sides. The sides of the door, carved out of the rock, are decorated with niches framed by half-columns and intended to

The Arch of the Siq by a drawing of Roberts (1839)

29

hold statues. It is not certain whether the structure had an exclusively monumental meaning, similar to that of Roman triumphal arches, or whether it had wooden doors actually capable of protecting the city from potential enemies.

The **Siq** unwinds for a length of over two kilometers until the point where it suddenly opens onto the rock façade of al-Khazneh. The rock walls of the Siq reach a maximum height of 80-90 meters: in some stretches they are just 3 meters apart, barely sufficient for permitting the passage of carriages; in other points they are farther apart, forming large widened areas, where there were probably rest areas for the caravans. Along the route it is still possible to see sections of the limestone slab pavement probably laid during the years after the Roman conquest. Two channels are engraved along the walls for the entire length; through these channels, replaced in some points by small stone walls holding terracotta pipes, the water coming from the 'Ain Musa springs was conveyed toward the city center.

The walls of the gorge are covered with sculptures, bas-reliefs, votive niches, inscriptions, and graffiti bearing witness to the continuous, centuries-long use of the Siq from the Nabatean period through to the late Roman Age, and revealing its dual nature as a ritual passageway and a trade route.

The sacred and ritual function of the route can be seen in the numerous betyls adorning the sides of the Siq. One of the most complete and complex examples is found about midway along the way where, on a cubical rock, an aedicule is carved and framed by half-columns and topped with a Doric frieze. The aedicule

The Entrance Arch to the Siq, reconstruction

contains two **betyls** side by side, the larger of which has a schematic representation of two eyes and a nose; they probably represent Dushara and al-'Uzza, the principle gods of the Nabateans. Betyls of smaller sizes and simpler shapes can be encountered all along the Siq, carved singly or in groups; some are placed inside simple niches, while others are part of a more elaborate architectural frame. Lacking

*Tunnel excavated in the rock to carry water
from wadi Musa to the city*

inscriptions, it is impossible to tell which gods they represent. While betyls, altars, and votive aedicules show the sacred nature of the road, its important commercial function is illustrated by the **bas-relief of the caravan** carved into the southern wall just beyond the monumental god block. Only the lower part of the bas-relief, discovered during the work recently done for organizing and fixing up the tour route, is still preserved, while the upper part is completely eroded; it depicts two men dressed in Greek garments, each leading two dromedaries. The sculpture

Detail of the caravan bas-relief carved in the southern wall of the Siq

is a faithful reproduction of the caravans that crossed the Siq in Nabatean and Roman times to bring their loads of precious goods into the city. ›

AL-KHAZNEH

At the end of its long path, the Siq suddenly opens onto the wide area dominated by the colossal façade of **al-Khazneh al-Faroun**. The name, which means "the Pharaoh's Treasury", has its origins in the belief, long rooted among the Bedouin tribes, that an unnamed pharaoh had hidden a treasure in the urn crowning the façade. This belief is the reason for the numerous bullet holes that have ruined the upper part of the monument, bearing witness to the repeated – as well as useless – attempts to take possession of the supposed treasure.

Al-Khazneh emerges from among all of Petra's

Glimpse of the Khazneh from the Siq

monuments not only because of its spectacular position at the end of the Siq, but also because of its exceptional state of preservation, owing to the fact that it is deeply set into the mountainside and thus protected from the erosion of the elements. Almost always shaded by the high rock walls surrounding it, the monument, facing eastward, is completely illuminated by the sun only in the early hours of the morning.

The façade of al-Khazneh, which measures 28 meters in width by 40 in height, was

The monumental façade of al-Khazneh, carved into the mountainside

Detail of the architectural decoration with floral capitals

Relief with a Dioscuros from the façade

created by cutting away the natural rock, and it has two levels. The lower level consists of a portico with six Corinthian columns: while the two central columns are freestanding, the two pairs of side columns project from the wall behind them and frame niches holding, at more than life size, two semi-nude figures accompanied by horses. The two youths have been identified as the Dioscuri, Castor and Pollux, sons of Zeus, venerated during Hellenistic and Roman times throughout the Mediterranean basin. The columns of the portico, topped by floral capitals, hold a frieze and a pediment decorated with plant motifs. The center of the pediment features a head of Medusa (*gorgoneion*), while the corner elements (acroters) show two sphinxes and a sun disk framed by spikes of wheat and two cornucopias, the symbol of the Egyptian goddess Isis.

The upper level is dominated in the center by a small round temple (*tholos*) framed by two projecting side blocks. These side blocks are decorated with half-columns and crowned by half-pediments with acroters shaped like sphinxes and eagles; on their fronts and internal sides they have aedicules decorated with female figures on tall pedestals. Thanks to their attire, consisting of a short tunic, and the carrying of an ax, these figures can be identified as Amazons, the mythical warrior women who came from Asia Minor.

In the deep niches separating the side blocks from the *tholos*, there are representations of winged Victories (*Nikai*). The *tholos*, surmounted by a conical roof crowned by an urn, is also decorated with half-columns framing aedicules. While the two side aedicules are decorated with figures of Amazons, the central one has a draped female figure holding a cornucopia, the symbol of abundance, in her left hand and a cup for libations (*patera*) in her right. The identification of this figure has long been controversial. Her attributes are, in fact, characteristic of both the Egyptian goddess Isis and the Hellenistic personification of Fortune (Tyche), both often identified with al-'Uzza. The overlapping between these two goddesses in the late-Hellenistic age is demonstrated by several vases produced in Alexandria, Egypt that depict

Isis-Tyche, and by rupestrian dedications and bas-reliefs of Petra in which Isis is associated with al-'Uzza.

While the façade of al-Khazneh is embellished with a rich architectural and sculptural decoration, the interior is characterized, as is usual in Nabatean architecture, by an extreme simplicity. Opening onto the vast atrium (*pronaos*) behind the columns are three richly decorated portals providing access to three sections. In the central section, with a square plan and entered by way of a staircase, there are three small rooms framed by aedicules; the two side sections, preceded by a sort of vestibule, are smaller in size and have completely bare walls. All the rooms were originally stuccoed.

The identification of the function of the internal rooms is closely connected to the problem, long debated, of the interpretation and dating of the monument. Although several scholars have proposed an interpretation of al-Khazneh as a temple, the prevailing theory is that it was probably the monumental tomb of one of the Nabatean kings. The use of the edifice as a tomb is suggested by the funerary symbols of the decorations, the arrangement of the central chamber, and the position of the monument along the main access route to the city but outside the actual urban area. The function of the two side rooms remains uncertain: it is possible that they were used for the funeral rites connected with the cult of the deceased ruler. Just as controversial is the dating of the building, which has been set at various points between the 2nd century BC and the 2nd century AD. Especially on the basis of the analysis of the architectural decoration, which shows features char-

acteristic of late-Hellenistic art, the most accredited theory today is that the monument was built in about the mid-1st century BC to hold the remains of Aretas III (85-62 BC) or Obodas II (62-59 BC). The question, however, has not yet been definitively solved.

The harmony of its proportions and its refined decorations make al-Khazneh the undisputed masterpiece of Nabatean architecture. The iconographic and ornamental details show close ties with the trends developed in the late-Hellenistic age in Alexandria, Egypt; it is thus believed that the monument was created with the contribution of sculptors of Egyptian origin or training, who worked alongside local craftsmen. The resulting style, harmonious and eclectic at the same time, makes al-Khazneh not only the most famous of Petra's monu-

Al-Khazneh, the northern door of the vestibule

39

ments, but the maximum expression of the artistic trend which has been defined, to use a modern term, "late Hellenistic Baroque".

THE STREET OF FAÇADES

Continuing in the direction of the city, we go through the part of the Wadi Musa valley known as the Outer Siq. This stretch of road that leads to the monumental center of Petra is also known as the **Street of Façades** because the scenic faces of the rupestrian tombs are aligned along the tall rock walls delimiting it. The tombs facing onto the street are of the most simple and widespread type in Nabatean funeral architecture, characteristic of all the vast necropolises scattered along the gorges surrounding the city

These monuments, characterized by a remarkable vertical development, can be classified among the "tower tombs" widely used throughout the entire region since very ancient times. However, while the tower funeral monuments known in Syria and Palestine have their own architectural volume, the Nabatean tombs are reduced to a simple façade on the rock wall. The organization of the façade is very simple: in the lower part there is a rectangular or trapezoidal door, sometimes surmounted by a horizontal groove which originally held a stucco cornice; the upper part is decorated with battlements arranged in onÇ or two rows of stepped crenellations. This kind of crenellated frieze is also characteristic of the funerary architecture of the Middle East; since it is particularly common in Assyria and Persia, the stepped tombs of Petra are sometimes called "Assyrian tombs". Rows of tombs

of this type, lined up at various heights along the rock walls of Jabal al-Khubtah, are visible to the right of the Street of Façades. Their uniform, monotonous appearance was originally enlivened by the plaster facing, now lost, which was colorfully painted yellow, red, and blue. The general scheme is sometimes enriched by the use of sober architectural decoration, generally limited to the enclosing of the door in a more or less elaborate frame, and the insertion of lesenes at the ends of the façade. The interior of the rupestrian tombs is extremely simple, consisting of an unadorned funeral chamber with burial niches cut into the walls.

Crenellated rupestrian tombs along the Street of Façades

The tower tombs with stepped crenellations are generally dated from the 1st century AD, on the basis of the few surviving inscriptions, and especially by virtue of the comparison with the funerary edifices of Hegra (a Nabatean outpost on the Arabian Peninsula, today's Medain es-Saleh in Saudi Arabia).

Contemporary with the monumental tombs of the Nabatean kings, the tower tombs have a strong local style, although sometimes combined with elements taken from the Greek-Roman decorative repertory. They were certainly the tombs of the flourishing Nabatean middle class, made up of craftsmen and merchants with respectable economic means and a conservative spirit, who preferred, unlike the kings and ruling class, cultural and artistic models more in keeping with Nabatean tradition.

THE THEATRE

The **theatre** stands at the eastern extremity of the urban area, at the point where the Wadi Musa gorge starts to open out into a wide valley. The building, which could seat between 6,000 and 8,000 spectators, is partly carved out of the northeastern slope of the Zibb 'Attuf massif, and partly built. The area of the tiered seats (*cavea*) is entirely dug out of the rock and consists of 45 rows of seats, divided into three horizontal sections (*moeniana*) by annular corridors (*diazomata*) and divided into six vertical sections (wedges) by staircases that provided access for the spectators. At the time of construction, the *cavea* included only the two lower *moeniana*, above which there ran a road onto which several rupestrian tombs faced. At a later time it was raised

in height in order to increase the theatre's seating capacity, and the road was demolished. Of the tombs that once overlooked the road, only the funeral chambers are still visible today, in the rock wall behind the theatre.

The semicircular space (orchestra) separating the *cavea* from the stage has a diameter of 25 meters and was also created by cutting into the natural rock. It is accessible at the sides by way of two vaulted corridors (*parodoi*), which were once plastered and painted. Unlike the cavea and the orchestra, the stage was completely built. The front of the stage (*pul-*

The Theatre seen from a dwelling carved into the wall of Jabal al-Khubtha pitum), 38 meters long, is decorated by niches, alternately rectangular and semicircular in shape. In the stage wall (*frons scaenae*), 54 meters long, and with only the lower part preserved, three doors can still be seen inserted in large niches flanked by aedicules: the largest one, in the middle, (*porta regia*) opens at the end of a large semicircular exedra, while the smaller ones on either side (*portae hospitales*) occupy rectangular niches. The entrances were originally flanked by projecting colonnaded volumes arranged on two levels, of which only the lower one remains. The stage was originally covered with marble and frescoes and the aedicules in the façade were decorated with statues.

The theatre layout is typically Roman and conforms perfectly to the canons laid down in the late 1st century BC by Roman architect Vitruvius for the construction of buildings for entertainment. This fact is all the more surprising if we consider that the theatre was built in the first half of the 1st century AD, in an age when the Nabatean kingdom had not yet fallen under Roman rule. During the last period of Nabatean independence, the enlightened guidance of king Aretas IV (9 BC-40 AD), who is credited with the construction of the theatre, permitted Petra, a cosmopolitan trade center, to receive and assimilate the best the Hellenistic East and Roman West had to offer in terms of artistic and cultural models. The theatre later underwent various restoration operations; the two most important were during the reign of Malichus II (40-70 AD) and during the period after the Roman conquest. It was precisely during this latter operation, which was carried out during the first half

Theatre, reconstruction of the stage and of the cavea

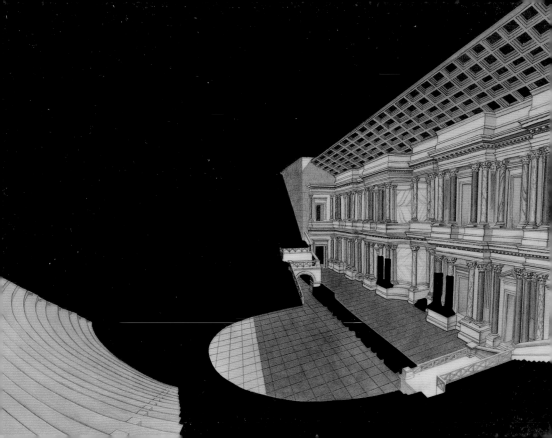

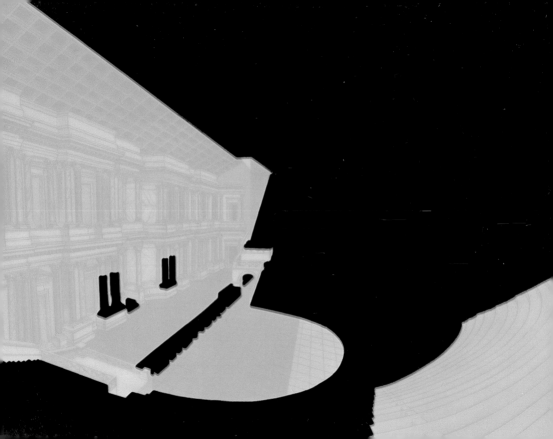

of the 2nd century AD, that the theatre was enlarged to the detriment of the road and the rupestrian tombs. The monument was abandoned after the disastrous earthquake of 363, which caused the stage to cave in.

The Theatre stage

The area where the theatre stands is at the eastern limit of the urban area. In the most ancient phase, when the city was limited to the central sector of the Wadi Musa valley, this area must have been suburban in nature, as demonstrated by the widespread presence of tombs. In a more recent phase, contemporary with and subsequent to the construction of the theatre, the expansion of the city entailed the transformation of this area into a residential area. This explains the presence of rupestrian dwellings in the Jabal al-Khubtah wall opposite the theatre: the largest and most intricate is a house made up of various rooms dug out of the rock, opening onto a central room that receives light from the outside. Similar dwellings, made up of communicating rooms dug out of the rock and originally decorated with stuccowork and frescoes, are visible in large numbers on the slopes of the rocky massifs delimiting the central sector of the Wadi Musa valley. They can be distinguished from the rupestrian tombs by the fact that they lack carved façades.

THE CENTRAL AREA

To the west of the theatre, there opens a wide canyon crossed by the Wadi Musa and delimited by the tall rocky Jabal al-Khubtah massifs to the east and the al-Habis plateau to the west.

In order to prevent the danger of sudden river floodings and, at the same time, guarantee a constant water supply, the course of the Wadi Musa was regulated with the construction of strong embankments and channeled through the creation of a complex system of water conduits. Furthermore, in order to ensure a

more effective defense of the city, wherever the natural protection of the rock was missing, wall sections equipped with towers were built. In the area to the north of the river it is still possible to see sizable parts of the wall, among which stand out the powerful foundations of a circular bastion known as the **Conway Tower**.

Inside the vast area delimited by the perimeter of the fortresses, rise the city's most important public and religious buildings, most of which are situated along the southern short of the *wadi*. The southern and northern slopes of the valley, which have not yet been studied, were probably occupied by the city's residential areas.

THE COLONNADE STREET

The valley is crossed for its entire length by a wide **Colonnade Street** running east-west and parallel to the course

Eastern face of the Temenos Gate: pilaster of the central arch showing vegetal motifs alternating with busts of deities

48

of the river. As has been verified by archaeological investigations, the street repeats the layout of an older cobblestone road, constructed in around the mid-1st century BC for the purpose of offering an adequate solution to the problem of the growing vehicular traffic that Petra had to cope with at the peak of its development as a caravan metropolis.

The Colonnade Street, constructed in the early 2nd century AD, is preserved for a maximum length of almost 300 meters. The street, 6 meters wide, is paved with marble and sandstone slabs and flanked by sidewalks on which stand sandstone columns. Of the seventy-two columns that originally made up the colonnade, nineteen have been recently repositioned on the southern side. The absence of furrows in the pavement indicates that the street was not used for vehicular traffic, but was of a prevalently ceremonial nature. The southern side was occupied, behind the colonnade, by an almost uninterrupted row of shops; on the northern side, on the other hand, the porticos probably served only to hide the irregularity of the buildings behind them.

Colonnade streets are a distinctive element in the urban planning of the large cities in the Roman East. Built during the golden age of the caravan trade in all the metropolises of the Syrian-Palestinian area (such as Apamea, Palmyra, Bosra and Gerasa), they place the urban layout of the major traffic arteries within a monumental architectural frame, and at the same time have a practical and representative purpose. The multiple functions of the Colonnade Street of Petra, as well as of the Nabatean street that preceded it, are seen in the buildings of a commercial, public, and religious nature that line it on the north and south sides.

Reconstruction of the Colonnade Street and of the Temenos Gate

The Colonnade Street with the Royal Tombs to the east

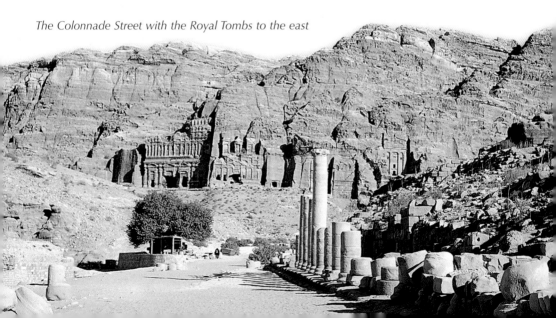

THE NYMPHAEUM

At the eastern extremity of the street, where the only tree offering some shade in the sun-drenched Wadi Musa Canyon grows today, there is a monumental public fountain (*nymphaeum*). The **nymphaeum** stands at the point where the Wadi Mataha flows into the Wadi Musa. It served simultaneously as a spectacular conclusion of the city aqueduct, and as a public fountain where caravans arriving in Petra could refresh themselves.

The nymphaeum, with a triangular plan, rose on three steps and consisted of a wall decorated with a large semicircular niche flanked by two smaller rectangular niches. The niches were probably decorated by statues and certainly framed by projecting columns on high bases.

Today only the lower steps remain of the sumptuous construction. The nymphaeum was built at the same time as the Colonnade Street, in the context of the major urban renewal operations that involved the entire central area in the early 2nd century AD.

On the opposite side of the street there are three vast adjoining open-air areas, generally referred to as the Upper Market, Central Market, and Lower Market.

The **Upper Market** and the **Central Market** have not been excavated, but their prevalently commercial use has never been in doubt. Yet to be verified, on the other hand, is the interpretation of the Upper Market as a large public square used for trade (*agora*). While the exact function of the Upper Market is still uncertain, its dating to the age of the emperor Trajan (98-117 AD) is confirmed by the inscription that appears on the base

Proposal of reconstruction of the Nymphaeum

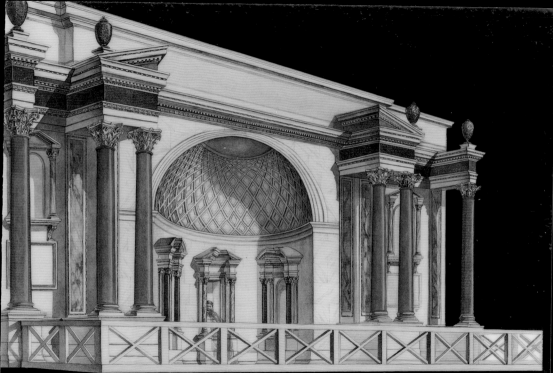

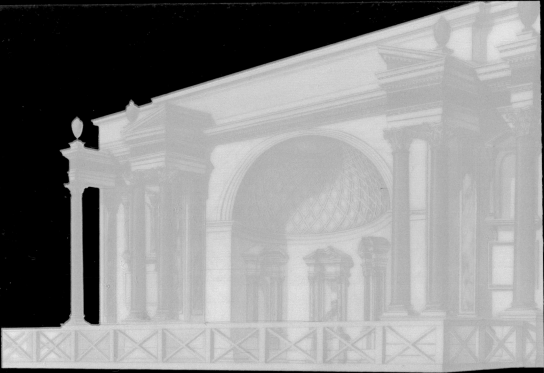

of the monumental arch, which is no longer standing today, and through which the complex was once entered. Along the front of the Upper Market and the Central Market is a long line of shops; dating from the age of the construction of the Colonnade Street, they were rebuilt after the earthquake of 363, partially encroaching upon the portico area.

Unlike the Upper Market and the Central Market, the **Lower Market** has been recently involved in archaeological studies that have definitively clarified its function. The complex is not a market at all, but instead a vast open-air area used as a garden and equipped with a pool. At the center of the pool, which measures 43 x 23 meters, stands a pavilion richly decorated with marble, stuccowork, and frescoes. Against the backdrop of arid rock that characterized the landscape of Petra, the gardens and pool certainly created an effect of extraordinary scenic impact. The complex was built toward the end of the 1st century BC.

THE SOUTH TEMPLE

To the west of the pool complex stands a large sanc-

Nabatean coin with the portrait of king Malichus I

tuary, known by the name of **South Temple** or Large Temple, which dominates the southern side of the Colonnade Street.

The South Temple can be reached from the street through a monumental door (*propylon*) and a double staircase, and is organized on two terraces, one over the other. The staircase leads to the lower terrace, measuring 49 x 56 meters, supported to the north by a heavy wall of square blocks and delimited on the sides by a triple colonnade. The columns, which total twenty in number, are surmounted by capitals decorated with elephant heads. The lower terrace served as a sacred enclosure for the temple (*temenos*) and was accessible to the faithful; the entrance to the upper terrace, on which the building of worship stood, was, instead, reserved for the priests.

At the center of the upper terrace stands the actual temple, preceded by an open-air courtyard and a monumental portico and flanked by two covered side passageways. The edifice, which occupies an area measuring 42.5 x 28 meters, consisted in an early phase of a vestibule (*pronaos*) with two columns between pillars, and an internal space (*cella*) delimited by columns on all sides. The columns, eight on the long sides and six on the back side, were surmounted by capitals with floral decorations. In a second phase the spaces between the columns were closed by walls, and inside a small theatre seating 600 was built. These substantial changes were made over just a few years' time. In fact, the temple was built in the late 1st century BC, and the *cella* was modified during the first half of the 1st century AD. Restored several times, the sanctuary remained in use up until the 6th century, when it was destroyed by an earthquake. The temple has a strong Eastern style, which can be seen in particular in the multiplication of the colonnaded courtyards, and shows considerable affinities with the contemporary sanctuaries in the Syrian and Palestinian area. The inclusion of a theatre inside the *cella* is an absolutely unprecedented touch, although the association between theatres and sacred buildings was a fairly common element in the sanctuaries of the Near and Middle East. The fact that that association was also customary in Petra is demonstrated by an inscription found inside the Byzantine church on the opposite shore of the Wadi Musa, which states that Aretas IV, in the eleventh year of his reign (2-3 AD), had dedicated a theatre and a sacred building to the god Dushara. Even though this cannot be tied with certainty to the South Temple, the inscription proves the existence, in the Nabatean world, of cult theatres, buildings in which sacred representations and religious rites connected with the cult were performed.

With its monumental dimensions and scenographic appearance, the South Temple is the largest discovered up to now in Petra. It must have thus been named after one of the most important city deities, but the theory that it was dedicated to al-'Uzza or Tyche is, at the present time, totally impossible to prove.

THE TEMPLE OF THE WINGED LIONS

Right across from the South Temple, on the opposite side of the Colonnade Street and on the northern bank of the Wadi Musa, stands another important sanctuary, called the **Temple of the Winged**

The South Temple, reconstruction

Relief showing Cupid with a winged lion

Lions after the characteristic form of its capitals. The building, situated on a plateau, was once reachable by crossing a bridge and going up a long porticoed road that made it possible to overcome the difference in level from the river.

The temple is made up of a vestibule accessible through two narrow side openings, and a large square chamber (*cella*) in the center of which there is a monumental altar. The walls of the *cella* are decorated with half-columns framing niches, corresponding to two rows of freestanding columns along the sides. The decoration of the interior, no longer preserved today, was very rich. The floor and lower part of the

Temple of the Winged Lions, reconstruction of the cella

The Temple of the Winged Lions is perhaps the best example of the eclecticism of Nabatean architecture: in fact, it combines an Eastern type plan, recognizable mainly in the arrangement of the *cella* and the style of the altar, with a decorative scheme of Hellenistic-Roman inspiration. A fragmentary inscription confirms that the building was built during the thirty-seventh year of the reign of Aretas IV (27-28 AD); destroyed by a fire between 110 and 114 AD, it was never rebuilt. In this case, also, the god to whom the sanctuary was dedicated is unknown.

The temple is surrounded by several rooms which were in part the priests' quarters and in part craftsmen's shops. To the east, on a large terrace overlooking the river, the remains of a large colonnaded courtyard and a monumental building can be seen; these are commonly called the **Royal Palace**, but the real function is not known.

THE TEMENOS GATE

At the western extremity of the Colonnade Street, a monumental gate affords access into the sacred enclosure (*temenos*) surrounding the city's main sanctuary, known with the name of Qasr al-Bint Faroun ("Palace of the Pharaoh's Daughter").
The **Temenos Gate** is the monumental entrance to the sanctuary, marking the passage into the sacred area and hiding its difference in orientation compared to the public quarter. It shows a design characteristic of the Roman triumphal arches, with a wider central passageway and two smaller side ones but, unlike the gates, it was originally closed with wooden doors, whose hinges turned in the sockets still

present in the threshold.

The gate is constructed of sandstone and has a triple-barrel-vault structure framed by pillars. On the western side, facing

toward the Qasr al-Bint, half-columns are set against the pillars, while on the eastern side, facing the Colonnade Street, the scenographic effect is increased by the insertion of four columns on a tall pedestal in front. The sculptural decoration was particularly rich on the eastern side. The side passageways were, in fact, flanked by a continuous frieze decorated with plant motifs, while the central vault is framed by a series of panels depicting floral elements and busts of deities. The current appearance of the gate, which collapsed during an earthquake, is the result of a recent restoration operation.

The chronology of the monument is very much debated and the dating proposals

Medusa head from the Qasr al-Bint area

Reconstruction of the west side of the Temenos Gate towards the Qasr al-Bint

range from the 1st century BC to the 3rd century AD. The most plausible hypothesis is that it was built during the 2nd century AD and, in any case, during a period after completion of the Colonnade Street. Excavations recently conducted in the area have, however, revealed that the gate replaced a more ancient entranceway, built at the same time as the temple.

Certainly pertaining to the original entrance to the sanctuary (of which only the foundations remain) are the two towers flanking the Roman construction. From the south tower a staircase leads to a group of underground buildings whose exact function still remains to be understood. These are three underground rooms, one with a circular plan and two rectangular, vaulted

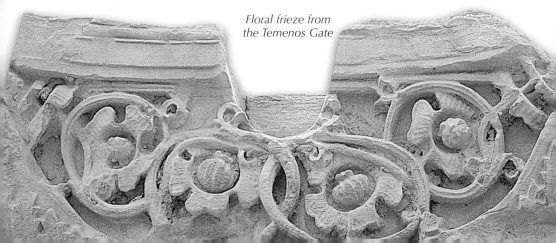

Floral frieze from the Temenos Gate

and decorated with half-columns, stuccoes, and frescoes. At the time of their discovery, they were interpreted as thermal bath structures but, since there are no signs of a water delivery or heating system, it is preferable to think of them as banquet rooms. A fascinating, but currently unverifiable, theory is that these rooms were part of a palace; also uncertain is their precise relationship with the nearby sanctuaries of the South Temple and the Qasr al-Bint.

The monumental gate leads into the vast sacred area (*temenos*) surrounding the **Qasr al-Bint** sanctuary. The *temenos*, ir-

Bust of Melpomene, muse of Tragedy, holding a mask

regular in shape because of the conformation of the land, is a spacious paved courtyard enclosed by walls and lined on all sides with benches. In the center of the courtyard there is a square, stepped monumental altar, about 3 meters high, originally faced with marble.

THE QASR AL-BINT

The Qasr al-Bint is the oldest and most important sanctuary in Petra. In fact, the current building, which dates from the 2nd half of the 1st century BC, stands over a previous place of worship.

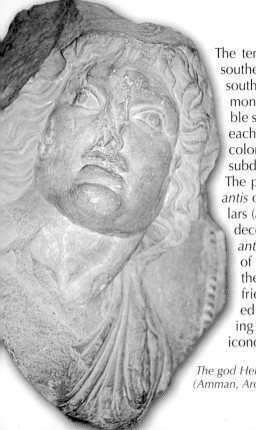

The temple stands on a tall platform (*podium*) in the southernmost part of the *temenos*, and on a north-south axis. Accessible on the north side by way of a monumental staircase consisting of twenty-two marble steps, the building is square, measuring 32 meters each side, and is 29 meters tall. It is made up of a colonnaded vestibule (*pronaos*) and an internal room subdivided into several smaller rooms.

The pronaos, wide and shallow, has four columns *in antis* on the front, i.e. situated between two corner pillars (*antae*); the *antae* are covered with stucco panels decorated with geometric elements in relief. The *antae* and the columns are surmounted by capitals of a floral style that recall those of al-Khazneh and the South Temple. Above the architrave, the Doric frieze is made up of triglyphs and metopes decorated alternately with rosettes and medallions containing busts of deities. The busts, mutilated during the iconoclast period, have completely disappeared; only

The god Helios, from the frieze of Qasr al-Bint.
(Amman, Archaeological Museum)

The Temple of the Qasr al-Bint, façade reconstruction

one specimen still survives, and is kept today at the Museum of Amman. It shows the god Helios (the Sun) and enables us to appreciate the exceptional quality of the sculptural decoration. The frieze, which was originally plastered and painted, is surmounted on the front by a triangular tympanum. The entire external perimeter of the temple was covered with gilded and painted stucco; traces of the original decoration with half-columns and aedicules in relief are still preserved on the rear wall of the building.

At the center of the back wall of the pronaos opens a wide, covered arch door that leads into the *cella*. It is divided into a rectangular front part, which occupies the whole width of the building, and a rear part, subdivided into three rooms. The central room is the *adyton*, i.e. the most sacred part of the sanctuary, in which the cult statue was kept. Raised about one and a half meters off the *cella* floor, it is accessible by means of two side flights of steps. The walls of the *adyton* had an elaborate stucco decoration, with half-columns supporting an architrave and figural frieze. The side rooms, opening onto the *cella* through two columns which originally supported a second floor, were probably used for cult banquets held in the deity's honor.

Like all the other sacred buildings of Petra, the Qasr al-Bint combines elements characteristic of eastern temple architecture (in particular, the square plan, the transverse orientation of the pronaos, and the stepped altar) and ornamental and sculptural details (such as Corinthian capitals, figural medallions, and stucco decorations) typical of the Hellenistic-Roman decorative repertoire. In this case, also,

the deity to whom the temple was dedicated has not been identified with any certainty.

The position, dimensions, and antiquity of the sanctuary make it very probable that the Qasr el-Bint was consecrated to the god Dushara. Probably built during the times of Obodas III (30-9 BC), the Qasr al-Bint underwent various restoration operations; damaged in the earthquake of 363, it was never rebuilt.

View of Qasr al-Bint with the Colonnade Street and the Royal Tombs in the background

THE ROYAL TOMBS

At the opposite end of the Wadi Musa valley, along the western slope of the Jabal al-Khubtah, there is a series of monumental tombs called the "Royal Tombs". The tombs, facing west and illuminated at sunset by the last rays of sunlight, offer a scenographic backdrop to the Colonnade Street. The theory that the tombs of al-Khubtah are the monumental tombs of the Nabatean kings has not, in reality, been proven by any document. On the other hand, their position, dimensions, and elaborate decorations make this

General view of the Royal Tombs along the western face of al-Khubtah

rated with half-columns that support an architrave decorated by four busts of deities (today almost completely illegible) and enriched by a lovely door surmounted by a Doric frieze and a small pediment.

The arrangement of the interior is very original, with one huge room on the ground floor and three adjoining rooms on the upper floor, corresponding to the openings visible on the upper part of the façade. The central opening still has its closing slab, decorated with a very badly worn male bust; the bust certainly represented the owner of the tomb, whom some identify as the Nabatean king Malichus II (40-70 AD). The rooms on the upper floor may thus be interpreted with certainty as funeral chambers. The room on the lower floor

The interior chamber of the Urn Tomb converted into a church, mid- 5th Century AD

The Urn Tomb with colonnade porticoes

an entirely reasonable possibility.

The southernmost of the royal tombs is the **Urn Tomb**, which takes its name from the large urn on top of its pediment. The tomb is preceded by a large open-air courtyard (21 meters wide) delimited on the sides by Doric colonnades dug out of the rock. During a late phase the courtyard was enlarged with the construction of a large platform supported by a system of barrel vaults which is still visible in front of the tomb. The façade, well developed in height, is deco was, instead, probably for holding the banquets and ceremonies held in honor of the deceased king. Its arrangement was profoundly changed in 446-447 when, as stated in the inscription painted on the back wall, the tomb was converted into a Christian church. The large arch-covered niches (arcosolia) seen on the back room of the room and the doors and open windows on the façade date from the Byzantine phase.

To the left of the Urn Tomb, in addition to a traditional Nabatean type tomb, there is the so-called **Silk Tomb**, so called because of the multicolored veins characterizing the bank of sandstone into which the façade is carved. The tomb, very damaged in the lower part, stands out for the simplicity and sobriety of its architectural decor, limited to the half-columns framing the door, the tall attic decorated with pillars, and the traditional stepped

The Silk Tomb façade

73

top. The only element worthy of note is the relief busts, almost completely obliterated by erosion, which decorate the side niches in the upper part of the façade.

THE CORINTHIAN TOMB

North of the Silk Tomb stands the monumental **Corinthian Tomb**, which takes its name from its Corinthian style floral capitals. Situated in a position particularly exposed to wind and water erosion, today the Corinthian Tomb is in a very poor state of preservation. The façade, 24.5 meters wide and 28 meters tall, is structured on two levels. The lower level

The Silk Tomb, detail of coloured bands in the rock

The Corinthian Tomb, reconstruction of the façade

is decorated, according to the traditional canons of Nabatean architecture, with half-columns framing niches and portals covered with alternating triangular and semicircular tympanums. On the floral capitals, now in bad state of preservation, rests the entablature, which opens in the center into a wide arch and is topped by a broken pediment. The first level reproduces the scheme of the upper level of al-Khazneh: the central *tholos*, surmounted by a conical roof, is framed by two projecting volumes topped by a tall attic and a broken pediment.

The doors and windows on the lower level are arranged asymmetrically. The central door leads into a large funeral chamber equipped with six burial niches. The two openings at the sides of the door were perhaps created during a phase of reuse of the room, while the two entrances north of the main portal lead into two smaller rooms.

In its attempt to assimilate the Hellenistic architectural canons and merge them with the local models, the Corinthian Tomb is one of the most original creations of Nabatean funerary architecture. The building's importance emerges clearly not only from its general structure, but also from its position, perfectly aligned with the Colonnade Street, of which it is a sort of ideal end. The monument was probably built during the second half of the 1st century AD to hold the remains of one of the last Nabatean kings, the members of his family, and their retinue.

THE PALACE TOMB

Immediately north of the Corinthian Tomb, the series of royal tombs ends with

The Palace Tomb, reconstruction

76

the most monumental of all the funerary buildings of Petra, which is called the **Palace Tomb** because of its resemblance to the homes of the Hellenistic rulers.

The façade, almost entirely carved out of the rock, is 49 meters wide and 45 meters tall, and consists of three levels, one above the other. The lower level, raised and originally accessible by means of steps cut into the rock, is entirely occupied by four colossal portals framed by elaborate architectural cornices. The second floor has a totally unusual structure: the façade is punctuated by nine pairs of half-columns, surmounted by Nabatean capitals, which support an entablature which alternates between projections and recesses. The model was certainly taken from the Hellenistic-Roman architectural tradition, in which half-columns are widely used, but reproduced without a real understanding of the structural value. Only the southern end of the façade of the third and last level, partly dug out of the rock and partly built, is preserved intact. It consists of an attic punctuated by vertically arranged rows of pillars repeating the rhythmic succession of the half-columns of the level below.

The four portals lead into four rooms lined with benches. The presence of benches and absence of burial niches show that these rooms served as tricliniums. The Palace Tomb is certainly the latest among all the Royal Tombs; it is believed that it may be the tomb of the last Nabatean king, Rabbel II (70-106 AD) but, as usual, the theory so far remains without proof.

Even if they do not really belong to the group of Real Tombs, the Tomb of 'Unaishu and Tomb of Sextius Florentinus, which occupy the south corner and north corner, respectively, of the western slope of Jabal al-Khubtah, are closely related to them from both a topographical and an ideological standpoint.

The Tomb of 'Unaishu, reachable by way of a path that branches off from the main itinerary near the Street of Façades and the theatre, is part of a group of three monumental funerary buildings occupying the slopes of the Jabal al-Khubtah opposite the theatre. The three tombs, of the tower type with stepped top, are of considerable size and very similar appearance; the tall, elegant façade framed by pillars is enriched by a door situated within an elaborate architectural frame. The **Tomb of 'Unaishu** is the southernmost of the three tombs and is preceded by a courtyard on which a funerary triclinium faces. Its interest lies in the inscription engraved on the closing slab (no longer preserved today) of the burial chamber, which makes it possible to identify the owner of the tomb as 'Unaishu, minister of Queen Shaqilat, mother of Rabbel II (70-106 AD), and to date the building between 70 and 76 AD. The dimensions, elegance, and position of the two rupestrian façades situated between the Tomb of 'Unaishu and the Urn Tomb authorize us to suppose that they, too, were built for high-ranking dignitaries of the Nabatean court.

THE TOMB OF SEXTIUS FLORENTINUS

At the opposite end of the western slope of the Jabal al-Khubtah, slightly distanced from the group of royal tombs, stands the **Tomb of Sextius Florentinus**, identified by the long inscription in Latin running along the entablature. As the inscription states,

Titus Aninius Sextius Florentinus was the governor (*legatus Augusti pro praetore*) of the province of Arabia under the emperor Hadrian between 127 and 130 AD; he died while still in office and had expressed in his testament that he wished to be buried in Petra. The tomb, built by his son according to his father's wishes, has a very elaborate façade. The lower part, severely damaged by erosion, is decorated with pillars and half-columns and by a door surmounted by a tympanum. The upper part consists of an attic with three vertically arranged rows of dwarf pillars

The Sextius Florentinus Tomb, detail of the arch

The Tomb of Sextius Florentinus, Roman governor of Arabia: reconstruction of the façade

and is topped by a triangular pediment. In the center of the attic there is a wide arch decorated with a head of Medusa surrounded by plant elements and surmounted by an eagle in relief. In spite of the persistence of several characteristics typical of Nabatean architecture, the tomb shows a strong Hellenistic-Roman style in its architectural development and sculptural decoration. The Tomb of Sextius Florentinus stands out from Petra's other funerary buildings also for the arrangement of its burial chamber, whose walls are decorated with half-columns and still preserve traces of the original stucco facing.

THE ZIBB 'ATTUF AND THE WADI AL-FARASA

The peak of Zibb 'Attuf, an imposing rocky massif rising south of the Wadi

Musa valfice. The sanctuary is reached from the ancient Sacred Way that branches off from the main route between the Street of Façades and the theatre, climbing up along the narrow Wadi al-Mahfu gorge. Ascending along the valley using numerous flights of steps cut into the rock, we reach a level area from which rise, at a distance of about 30 meters, two colossal **obelisks** cut out of the rock. The significance of the two obelisks is not entirely clear, but by virtue of the shape and size and, especially, the proximity to the high place, it is generally believed that they are colossal god blocks depicting Dushara and al-'Uzza.

From the area of the obelisks a steep

View of the two obelisks in proximity of the high place of Zibb 'Attu

staircase leads to the level peak of the Zibb 'Attuf, also known by the name of Jabal al-Madhbah, i.e. "sacrifice hill". Here stands the most vast and important of Petra's high places, from which a spectacular view of the city's center and surrounding mountains can be enjoyed. Situated on a large level area, the sanctuary consists of a cult triclinium delimited by a low step, in the center of which there is a sacred table on which the offerings for the gods were placed. West of the triclinium and across from the table stand the sacrifice altar, preceded by three steps, and, to the left, a circular altar for libations, complete with

The high place on the summit of Jabal al-Madhbah, "the Mount of the Sacrifice"

drainage channel. A small cistern situated near the altars was perhaps used to wash and purify the instruments used for the sacrifices. Numerous other cisterns were situated near the sanctuary; they were used to collect the rainwater used in the sacred ceremonies.

The Zibb 'Attuf is delimited to the west by the deep Wadi al-Farasa gorge, along which some of Petra's most interesting tombs are found. A steep, narrow path skirting the obelisk area leads down from the Jabal al-Madhbah to the Wadi al-Farasa valley. This route, also, must have been a sacred way in ancient times, as suggested by the religious inscriptions and engraved god blocks along the road. At the point where the path turns toward the bottom of the gorge, on the rock is carved the monumental figure of a lion, 4 meters wide and 2.5 meters tall; some traces of channeling indicate that the monument was, in reality, a fountain. Since the lion is often associated with the goddess al-'Uzza, the **Fountain of the Lion** may have also had a cult significance.

The Fountain of the Lion along the path descending towards wadi Farasa

The first monument encountered on the descent along the Wadi al-Farasa is the so-called **Garden Tomb**, which owes its name to the luxuriant vegetation that covered the building at the time of its discovery. The

The Garden Tomb

The Roman Soldier Tomb

appearance of the Garden Tomb is total-ly unusual and has led scholars to sup-pose, in spite of its name, that it is not a funerary building, but a temple or a tri-clinium. The simple façade, composed of two columns situated between pillars, stands out against the backdrop of a wide courtyard. The portico leads into a vestibule onto which a square room opens. The heavy wall delimiting the courtyard forms the southern limit of a large cistern (18 x 9 meters) opposite which there is a room, once vaulted, dec-orated with niches and probably used for banquets.

Continuing beyond the Garden Tomb, we come across one of the most vast and unique funerary complexes of Petra. A vast open-air area, whose limits are marked by the walls of the gorge, separates two buildings carved into the rock: the **Roman Soldier's Tomb**, which takes its name from the figure carved above the door, and the funerary triclinium across from it. The tomb, dating from between the late 1st and early 2nd century AD, offers a good example of the mixture between the typical characteristics of the Nabatean funerary architecture and the styles of representation typical of the Hellenistic-Roman culture. The façade, topped by a triangular tympanum, resembles the front of a temple. The portal is soberly framed by lesenes surmounted by a Doric frieze and a small triangular pediment. The most interesting elements are the figures decorating the three niches situated in the upper part of the façade: the central niche contains the male figure wearing armor that gives the tomb its name; the side niches show two youths wearing a short tunic. The sculptures probably depict the deceased – perhaps a high-ranking officer of the Roman army stationed in Petra – and his sons, according to an iconography typical of Roman funerary reliefs. The interior of the tomb consists of two adjacent funeral chambers, the larger of which has burial niches carved into the walls.

Opposite the Roman Soldier's Tomb, beyond the open-air area that must have originally been adorned with porticoes, rises a vast funerary **triclinium**. The front, originally opened by three doors surmounted by windows, has been completely eroded by water. The large interior room, measuring 10.5 meters each side, is, instead, perfectly preserved. The walls, lined on three sides with benches, are rhythmically punctuated by rectangular niches framed by half-columns. The splendid red, white, and blue veins of the sandstone into which the room is dug were originally hidden by plaster. The elegant decoration of the room, an *unicum* in Petra's architecture, takes its inspiration from the reception halls of Hellenistic palaces and Roman *domus*, in which the walls were often airily opened by windows decorated with architectural frames. Having left behind the Roman Soldier's Tomb, the Wadi al-Farasa widens into a large valley and the path cut into the rock becomes an actual road. In the wall of the Zibb 'Attuf, which delimits the valley, are carved various rupestrian tombs at various levels, most of which are of the customary tower type. Two buildings, known respectively with the names of Renaissance Tomb and Broken Pediment Tomb, stand

Funerary Triclinium of the Roman Soldier Tomb, detail of the interior

The Renaissance Tomb

out from the others and deserve particular attention.

The **Renaissance Tomb** has a façade framed by pillars and is topped by a pediment supporting urn-shaped acroters. The distinctive element, which gives the tomb its name, is the wide arch that finishes the door frame at the top, which resembles that of the Tomb of Sextius Florentinus and recalls the creations of the Italian Renaissance.

A few meters further down, at the top of a staircase cut into the rock, is the **Broken Pediment Tomb**, which reproposes, with several variations, the general scheme of the pediment tomb. The door, severely damaged, is recessed and framed by two projecting volumes set off by pairs of pillars, to which the two half-pediments forming the "bro-

ken pediment" giving the tomb its name correspond at the top.

THE JABAL AD-DAYR

The ascent to Jabal ad-Dayr, along the path of the ancient sacred way that reached the large rupestrian sanctuary of ad-Dayr, is one of Petra's most fascinating itineraries. The path, which starts near the museum, climbs in the first part along the bottom of a narrow gorge and then goes up the crags of the Jabal ad-Dayr until it reaches the top. The route offers one of the most beautiful panoramas over the Wadi Musa valley and the Royal Tombs.
A branch-off from the left of the path leads to a group of buildings looking

Stairway carved in the rock leading to Jabal ad-Dayr

over a small valley. These are two rupestrian tombs with very simple façades and a funerary triclinium, which is called the **Triclinium of the Lions** after the animals carved at the two sides of the door. The façade is enriched by a gilded Doric frieze decorated at the ends by two Medusa heads and a pediment decorated with plant motifs. The interior room is lined with benches. The sober, refined style of the decoration has led scholars to date the triclinium to the golden period of Nabatean art, in the early 1st century AD.

The summit of Jabal ad-Dayr with the largest of Petra's rock-cut monuments

Continuing along the path, which unwinds across flights of steps carved into the rock, after going past several caves used during Christian times as hermitages, we arrive at the large clearing dominated to the east by the colossal rupestrian façade of **ad-Dayr**.

The monument, 40 meters tall and 50 meters wide, is carved into the western slope of the peak of Jabal ad-Dayr: set deeply into the mountain and protected from the erosion of the elements, it has remained practically intact. The façade is structured into two vertically arranged rows. The lower row is delimited by pillars and punctuated by half-columns; the two central half-columns frame an aedicule in which the portal topped by a tympanum is inserted; at the sides of the portal are symmetrically arranged two niches topped by small semicircular pediments. The upper row is a schematic

Ad-Dayr, detail of the upper order

reproduction of the al-Khazneh model: a central *tholos* with a conical roof surmounted by an urn and two projecting side volumes topped with half-pediments, decorated by large niches delimited by half-columns with Nabatean capitals. At the ends are two pillars paired with half-columns. A continuous Doric frieze, with triglyphs and disks in the metope field, ties together all of the architectural elements of the second level. Although the Hellenistic elements of al-Khazneh appear here interpreted according to a

The imposing rupestrian façade of ad-Dayr

92

local taste, ad-Dayr is perhaps the façade in Petra that best illustrates, in the essentiality of its lines and in its strong chiaroscuros, in the contrast between the concave and convex surfaces, that concept of "Hellenistic Baroque" that is generally applied to Nabatean architecture.

From the portal, once preceded by a staircase, we enter a vast square room measuring 11 meters each side, with two benches on the sides. On the back wall there is an aedicule framed by pillars, which preserves traces of the original stucco decoration; in the cavity behind it there is an altar reached by small flights of steps on the side. The arrangement of the interior chamber indicates clearly that ad-Dayr was a place of worship where ceremonies and banquets were held, perhaps a commemorative monument consecrated to the memory of a Nabatean ruler deified after his death. The identification of this ruler is, of course, connected with the problem of the monument's chronology, which is set somewhere between the mid-1st century BC and the late 1st century AD. The large area in front of the building was originally closed by a colonnaded portico of which only a few column sections remain to the right of the façade. The portico delimited a large sacred area used for large gatherings that were held on the occasion of religious celebrations.

As shown by the crosses cut into the sides of the niche inside the room, ad-Dayr was converted during a late period into a building for Christian worship. It is precisely this transformation that gave the monument its name, which means "the Monastery".

The numerous installations of a religious nature (cisterns, platforms, votive aedi-

cules, rupestrian rooms, actual sanctuaries) that punctuate the Jabal ad-Dayr indicate that this mountain was a place particularly venerated by the inhabitants of Petra.

THE BYZANTINE BASILICA

Although the city's most well-known monuments date from Nabatean and Roman times, Petra was also a thriving center in the early Byzantine age, before the Arab invasions brought about its final abandonment. Evidence of the Byzantine occupation of Petra can be seen both in the conversion into churches of monuments such as the Urn Tomb and ad-

Mosaics of the Byzantine Church: medallion with a dromedary

Dayr, and in the numerous crosses carved in various places throughout the city. The Mughar an-Nasara Plateau, which dominates the Wadi Musa valley to the north, holds in its name the distant memory of the Christian occupation: in fact, "Nasara" means "Nazarene", the term commonly used by the Arabs to indicate the Christians.

The building that best illustrates the prosperity reached by the Christian community of Petra between the 5th and the 6th century is the large Byzantine basilica – discovered in 1973 and only recently brought to light – situated north of the Wadi Musa valley right below the southern slopes of the Mughar an-Nasara.

The **basilica,** set on an east-west axis and covering an area measuring 25x16

Personification of Summer in the mosaic of the south aisle of the Byzantine basilica

meters, is preceded by a square atrium surrounded by porticoes, and is accessible through a portal flanked by lovely figural reliefs coming from ancient buildings. Inside, the basilica is divided into a nave and two aisles by two rows of eight columns each; the nave and aisles end in semicircular apses closed by marble barriers decorated with crosses. The mosaic decoration covering the floors of the nave and aisles is extraordinary. While the marble inlay flooring (*opus sectile*) of the nave has been almost completely removed, the large mosaic floors of the side aisles are perfectly preserved. The mosaic of the north aisle is made up of thirty circular medallions formed by vine branches emerging from an amphora flanked by two peacocks. The medallions are decorated with objects (amphorae, vases, candelabra), birds, animals, and human figures. The mosaic of the south aisle, partly damaged, has a central row of large rectangular medallions depicting the personifications of the Four Seasons, the Ocean, the Earth, and Wisdom, identified by short captions in Greek, while the side medallions, circular or square in shape, contain human figures and animals. The basilica was built during the 5th century and destroyed shortly after by a violent fire that broke out because of an earthquake, perhaps the one in 551. It is precisely the collapse of the roof onto the floor that ended up preserving the mosaics from the action of the atmospheric elements and attacks of the iconoclasts, allowing them to survive up to the present day.